WELCOME TO THE WORLD OF
Squirrels

Diane Swanson

Whitecap Books
Vancouver / Toronto

Edited by Elizabeth McLean
Cover design by Steve Penner
Interior design by Margaret Ng
Typeset by Maxine Lea
Photo research by Tanya Lloyd
Cover photograph by Thornley Woods, Tyne & Wear/firstlight.ca
Photo credits: Thomas Kitchin/firstlight.ca iv; Robert Lankinen/firstlight.ca 2, 10, 22; Wayne Lynch 4, 14; Tim Christie/timchristie.com 6, 16, 26; Mark Degner 8; Photo Bank Yokohama/firstlight.ca 12; Mary Clay/Dembinsky Photo Assoc 18, 20, 24.

Printed and bound in Canada

National Library of Canada Cataloguing in Publication Data

Swanson, Diane, 1944–
    Welcome to the world of squirrels

    Includes index.
    ISBN 1-55285-259-8

    1. Squirrels—Juvenile literature—North America. I. Title.
QL737.R685S838 2001   j599.36'097   C2001-910983-0

For more information on this series and other Whitecap Books titles, visit our web site at www.whitecap.ca

The publisher acknowledges the support of the Canada Council for the Arts and the Cultural Services Branch of the Government of British Columbia for our publishing program. We acknowledge the financial support of the Government of Canada through the Book Publishing Industry Development Program for our publishing activities.

Contents

World of Difference

SPOT A FURBALL RACING ALONG A BRANCH—and you've likely found a tree squirrel. It's a little rodent with a big bushy tail. Like other rodents, including beavers, porcupines, rats, and mice, the squirrel has sharp front teeth designed for gnawing. And it uses them often to crack open nuts.

Tree squirrels belong to a huge family of about 260 squirrels worldwide. It includes ground squirrels, prairie dogs, marmots, even chipmunks. In North America, there are 9 main kinds of tree squirrels: eastern and western gray, red, fox, Douglas, Abert's, Arizona gray, and northern and southern

This good-sized fox squirrel holds its long, thick tail up high.

1

flying squirrels. The biggest of these is the fox squirrel. Nose to tail, it can be as long as a woman's leg. The smallest—the southern flying squirrel—may be just a third that long!

Don't let the names of tree squirrels fool you. Gray squirrels can also be black, tan, or brown. Reds can also be gray or tan. And individual squirrels are usually different shades at

A flying squirrel peeks out of its home before it takes off.

different times of the year. What's more, flying squirrels don't really fly. They glide by using side flaps of skin that join their front and back legs. When these squirrels leap from trees, they just stretch out their legs, pull the flaps tight, and glide.

Because flying squirrels are active at night, they have large eyes that see well in the dark. Other tree squirrels are daytime animals. Their sight is about as good as a person's, but squirrels can see in more directions at once.

Squirrels often surprise people. Here are just some of the reasons why:

- A gray squirrel can run along a telephone wire, even while carrying two or three large nuts.
- A red squirrel can fall more than 30 metres (100 feet) to the ground without hurting itself.
- Squirrels can swim. Air trapped in their fur—especially on their tails—helps them float.

Where in the World

A soft rag can make a perfect lining for a squirrel's nest.

DON'T GO TO AUSTRALIA TO SEE TREE SQUIRRELS—or Antarctica, either. But you can find them on all the other continents on Earth.

Tree squirrels mostly make their homes in trees—inside holes and in nests on branches. Red squirrels might also use holes in the ground or in stone heaps, log piles, and rotting stumps. Southern flying squirrels sometimes move into sheds, cabins, and birdhouses.

Many tree squirrels have at least three homes each. Some have ten! Having more than one shelter helps squirrels avoid pests

such as fleas, escape enemies such as owls, and live close to the food they're gathering.

Nests on tree branches are usually used during warm weather. Squirrels such as grays and reds might fix up empty bird nests, but most build their own. Using leaves and twigs, they can weave a nest in a day. Then they curl up inside, where

When popping in and out of holes, squirrels use whiskers to help sense the size.

6

they've added a lining of moss or other soft materials.

When the weather turns cold, many tree squirrels move into tree holes. They might nibble around the entrances to enlarge them, then line the insides. A flying squirrel may take over a cluster of tree holes—one hole as a food cupboard, another as a bathroom, and a third as a nursery.

In winter, some squirrels share their homes with other squirrels. Snuggling together helps them stay warm.

RAIN FOREST ROUNDABOUT

Rain forests in North America help northern flying squirrels survive—and the squirrels help these forests grow.

Here's what happens: The squirrels eat a lot of truffles, potato-shaped fungi that grow underground. As they gather the fungi, the squirrels spread the seedlike spores that produce new truffles. The truffles help the roots of trees take in nutrients from the soil. And the trees provide northern flying squirrels with places to nest.

World in Motion

SPEEDING TREE SQUIRRELS ARE HARD TO CATCH—even on the ground. Moving their strong back legs together, they can hop away fast. But they seldom hurry from danger by heading in a straight line. Instead, they rush from the base of one tree or bush to the base of another, then another.

Tree squirrels are also great climbers. Sharp curved claws on each of their four feet help squirrels grip bark on trees—or bricks on buildings. And their toes are good at clutching branches or wires.

Squirrels dash along narrow branches

The long skinny toes of a Douglas squirrel cling easily to a narrow branch.

9

**Off and away!
A flying squirrel
g-l-i-d-e-s through
the air.**

as easily as they bolt across the ground. Their long tails help them balance. When they reach the end of one branch, they simply leap to another—or drop to the ground. Flattening their bodies, they spread out their legs and tails and fall gently, like parachutes.

Flying squirrels are the best gliders.

Using their special side flaps of skin, they easily sail 10 metres (30 feet) from place to place. If necessary, they can cover three to five times that distance in a single glide! By angling their tails and legs, they can turn in the air to avoid hitting trees, bushes, or anything else in their way.

A flying squirrel usually picks out its landing spot before it sets off. As it gets close, it slows down by lowering its back end and raising its tail. Then, thump! It lands softly on all four feet.

TAKING THE BRIDGE

Squirrels are quick, but cars are quicker. That's why traffic often strikes squirrels crossing city streets.

In Longview, Washington, one man was so concerned about squirrel safety that he built a special bridge across a busy road. Just wide enough for squirrels, Nutty Narrows Bridge stretched 18 metres (60 feet) from tree to tree. The man attracted squirrels to the bridge by sprinkling it with peanuts and setting up feeders in the middle and at each end.

World Full of Food

FRUIT AND NUTS MAKE GREAT SQUIRREL MEALS. Many squirrels also eat plant buds, mushrooms, insects, inner layers of tree bark, sweet sap, and eggs. Some feed on young birds and rabbits—and on antlers shed by male deer.

Squirrels search around trees for food, but those that live near people also find other places to hunt. They climb up back-yard poles and steal seed from birdfeeders. They wander around parking lots, picking dead insects off the headlights and bumpers of cars. One squirrel even ate candy canes hanging on a Christmas tree!

This Abert's—or tassel-eared—squirrel digs out dinner buried in the snow.

Red squirrels often snip cones off branches, then gather them up in heaps.

Most tree squirrels carry their meals to eating spots or store them somewhere for later use. They bury food such as nuts in the ground, digging shallow holes with their front feet. Then they pop in the food and cover it up by pushing soil and leaves with their feet and noses. It's possible for a red squirrel to live for up to two years on what it has stashed away. But it usually eats fresher meals.

Instead of burying their food, flying squirrels often store it in cracks in trees or tuck it under loose bark. Squirrels that eat mushrooms normally place them on branches to dry before stuffing them into holes in tree trunks.

Finding the food they've stored is seldom a problem for tree squirrels. They just sniff it out. Not only can they smell buried nuts, squirrels can even tell if insects have invaded the food.

DOING WHAT COMES NATURALLY

Squirrels don't have to learn how to hide the nuts they gather. It's something they do just by following their instincts —natural behaviors they're born with.

Even squirrels raised in cages have these instincts. The first time they're given nuts, they try to dig holes in the bottom of their cages. Then they shove the nuts into the imaginary holes and work their paws around as if they're covering the nuts with soil or leaves.

15

World of Words

"TCHRRR! TCHRRR! TCHRRR!" cries a red squirrel from its treetop location. It's telling a large gray squirrel down below to take off. "Tchrrr! Tchrrr! Tchrrr!" the red squirrel repeats, stressing the message by stomping its feet and twitching its tail.

Red squirrels are especially bold, but most tree squirrels scold whatever enters their feeding territories. A Douglas squirrel calls out—again and again—each day to make sure everyone knows where its territory is.

Squirrels also speak up to warn their young to behave. And if the little ones

What a chatterbox! No wonder red squirrels are also called barking squirrels and boomers.

are threatened or attacked, they cry out for help.

Not all squirrels make the same sounds. Fox and Abert's squirrels, for instance, cluck and bark in low voices. Gray squirrels usually sound scratchy, and they "click" when excited. Flying squirrels normally whistle or chirp—like birds—but squeak when bothered.

Not all talk is noisy. These two squirrels are giving each other a silent nuzzle.

All this talk is backed up by a squirrel's fluffy tail. The more excited or upset the squirrel feels, the more it flicks and twitches its tail.

Tree squirrels also deliver silent messages. They use smells for marking territories so that other squirrels stay away. Some of the smells come from sweat and oil glands in the animals' paws. A squirrel that's pulling itself along a tree branch may be spreading its odor with its front feet.

SOUNDING THE ALARM

Early one morning, a fox squirrel was nibbling nuts in a tree. Suddenly it barked and flicked its thick tail. The squirrel had spotted a bobcat on the ground below.

As long as the wild cat sat still, the fox squirrel was quiet. But whenever the cat stood up, the squirrel barked. It flicked its tail so fast that the tail whirled in circles. But the night's hunt had been good to the bobcat, and it simply walked away. Once again, the fox squirrel was quiet.

New World

TREE SQUIRRELS ARE BORN HELPLESS. They can't see or hear. They don't have fur to keep them warm. And many are so tiny that they each weigh less than a house key. Newborn flying squirrels weigh just half that!

A mother squirrel stays with her new pups as much as she can, leaving the nest only to feed herself. Often she has a family of three to care for. Curling up with the pups, she warms them with her body heat and feeds them her milk. Their whiskers help the newborns feel around for her.

Newborn squirrels snuggle to stay warm while their mother is out for lunch.

21

Although a mother squirrel isn't large, she defends her family fiercely. She attacks almost anything that threatens her young—even a snake or raccoon. And if she must, she'll move the pups to a safer home. She carries them one by one in her mouth, clutching them by the belly. Flying squirrels are able to airlift their young by gliding.

In their new fur coats, these squirrel pups are eager to leave the nest.

By the time the pups are about three weeks old, they're covered with a layer of fur. Soon they begin to hear, then to see. But until they're able to groom themselves, their mother licks them clean.

Bit by bit, squirrel pups start eating snacks such as grass, which their mother brings to them. And when they're about two months old, they can live without her milk. They spend more and more time out of the nest and begin to search for their own food.

Not all quacking comes from ducks. When it's time for tree squirrels to mate, females often call to males: "Quack, quack, quack." They also produce special smells to attract partners.

Male squirrels may fight over females, but they seldom hurt one another. They chase their mates until the females accept one—or sometimes more—of them. But mating squirrels don't stay together. Newborns never know their father.

Small World

PLAYING KEEPS YOUNG TREE SQUIRRELS BUSY. They chase one another around and around, and leap on rolling pine cones. All the exercise helps them grow strong.

Their mother encourages the pups to climb and follow her along tree branches. They practice jumping from the tip of one branch to the tip of another.

Flying squirrels need no flying lessons. They just start gliding naturally when they're about three months old.

With time and practice, squirrel pups improve their eating style. Red squirrels,

Ready, set, JUMP! A fox squirrel is hard at play.

for instance, grab hazelnuts at first sight and gnaw on them until the shell happens to crack open. Gradually, they discover that it's best to wear a groove in one side of the shell, jam their teeth into the nut, and break it into two chunks.

Pups also practice grooming themselves—something that squirrels do often, especially after

Even a birdhouse can become a new home for a young squirrel.